Photographs by Mitsuaki Iwago

ENGLISH EDITION
Executive Editor/Seiji Horibuchi
Publisher/Masahiro Oga

JAPANESE EDITION
Editor/Shuji Shimamoto
Art Director/Keisuke Konishi

Originally published in 1993
as *Nature Calls* by Shogakukan, Inc., Tokyo, Japan

ISBN 0-929279-95-6

First English Edition, 1993
10 9 8 7 6 5 4 3 2

Cadence Books
A Division of Viz Communications, Inc.
P.O. Box 77010
San Francisco, California 94107

NATURE CALLS

Mitsuaki Iwago's
Earthy Wildlife Photographs

Cadence Books

One creature's poop
is
another's manure

A black rhinoceros marks his territory

In the case of the African elephant, a lot goes in and a lot goes out

It's always soft after a meal of fresh meat

A male koala descends from the trees to mark his territory.
He sniffs the ground with a solemn expression

A cheetah preparing for the hunt takes care of business on a nearby anthill

A lion's morning toilet

The jet-spray style of the black rhinoceros

The zebra's is more like a faucet opened all the way

The African elephant's "fifth leg"

The African elephant's travels some ten feet before landing

Twilight. A black rhinoceros marks off his territory before heading home

Cattle egrets tag along, snatching up bugs as they go

A jackal cleans every bit of meat off a bone

The spotted hyena even eats the bones. Its droppings are made white by the calcium

A lion cub shows interest in urination

A herd of gnu gather on a lush Serengeti plain.
Their whiskers and their urine glisten, backlit by the setting sun

This gnu calf doesn't seem interested in urination

Silver gulls can be found on the same beaches as Australian sea lions

An ostrich's droppings blown in the wind

The color of an Adelaide penguin's droppings depends on what it eats

The black-legged kittiwake must raise its young
before the brief Arctic summer ends

A path leading from the nesting ground of
penguins to the sea is marked by droppings

The droppings of harp seals return to the sea when the ice melts

The frozen sea is kept in constant motion by the wind and the ocean currents

A Weddell seal's hole links the land and the sea

A trail of droppings left by a herbivore punctuates a dried marsh floor

A seal eats a penguin

A hippopotamus scatters its feces with its flat tail

Bat guano builds up like a thick, black carpet on the floor of a cave

A mold grows on some of the feces

Morning in the rainy season

A Thompson gazelle munches on a tender shoo

A buffalo's dropping is nearly a foot in diameter and more than an inch thick

An elephant's droppings set into motion by a crowd of dung beetles

A female grand gazelle announces with her scent that she is in heat

A giraffe scatters the seeds of an acacia with droppings

A zebra is able to digest even the toughest grasses

Marking one's territory is an important job

That's "number two" above and "number one" below

A female sambar

A female gnu

Just one day before this lion was hunting a buffalo

A male grand gazelle

A female buffalo

Mother and child take care of business on the same thicket

In the evening the hippopotamus comes out of the water to graze

The African elephant drinks between twenty and sixty-five gallons of water each day

The temperature in the desert can go as high as 120° F

A red kangaroo digs a hole to rest in

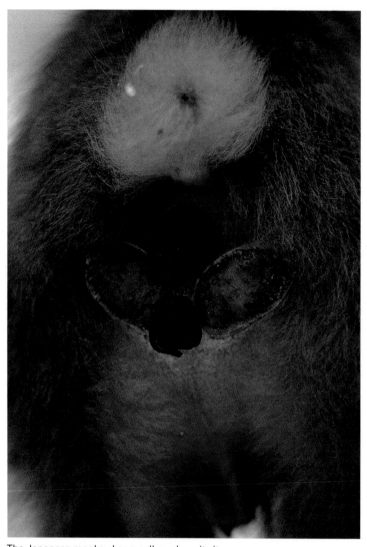

The Japanese monkey has a callus where it sits.

Beware of tree-borne monkeys

Baboons looking for beetles in elephant droppings

A gnu's feces burning in a field fire

 A scarab lays its eggs on a ball of dung. When the larvae hatches, it will eat the dung

An African elephant's raises mushrooms

The Masai make their huts from the manure and feces of cows

And once again, they eat

The rhythm of nature is
magnaminous

When Nature Calls

Mitsuaki Iwago

MITSUAKI IWAGO

Internationally acclaimed nature photographer Mitsuaki Iwago has traveled to some of the world's most remote regions. His 1986 book *Serengeti* has since become a worldwide bestseller; other works include *A Letter From the Ocean, A Letter From a Savanna, The Ocean of Whales, Penguin Continent* and *Kangaroo Time.* Despite his success, Iwago still spends most of his time in the natural habitats where wildlife thrives.

While attending the Frankfurt Book Fair, the editor of this book, Shuji Shimamoto, and I visit the Museum of Modern Art after a lunch of frankfurters. Since I spend much of my time in the wild, I look forward to this kind of occasional urban stimulation.

On first entering Frankfurt's Museum of Modern Art, one experiences the sensation of being enveloped in a wondrous space. The ceilings, walls, and stairs combine to divide up the space impressively. Moving from object to object, one is gradually overcome by a feeling of tranquillity and a heightening of the senses. At last Shuji and I find ourselves standing in front of a piece by Josef Boyce.

The title of the piece is "Blitzschlag mit Lichtschein aut Hirsch," which might be roughly translated as, "The thunderbolt that falls along with the shining of the light above the stag." A large steel triangle hangs on a wall, and scattered across the floor are thirty or so brown lumps, ranging between one and two feet in diameter. These brown lumps are so realistic that anyone who sees them must imagine the same thing.

"It looks just like dinosaur turds," says Shuji.

"Feces, too, can become art," I respond.

"Come to think of it, there were pictures of feces in your book *Serengeti,* too."

"You know what they say...'nature calls.'"

"Eating, defecating, giving birth. Wild animals really live by instinct, don't they?"

By the time our conversation is over we decide to make a book that portrays that reality frankly.

The two of us part in Frankfurt and I fly off to Africa to photograph lions. Lions may look as if they're sleeping all the time, but actually they're just resting quietly. In the evening, as the sun sinks in the west, diagonal rays of light vividly enhance the color of the sky and the grass. The female lions roll around, twist their bodies, yawn and stand up. They stretch out their forelegs, yawn again, and then begin to steadily scan the horizon. The expression on the lions' faces at this moment is my favorite. It's as if they're doing warm-up exercises to prepare for the hunt, tension gradually building in the muscles of their bodies. Somewhere in the distance a spotted hyena howls, and the females move their ears as if irritated by the sound. They yawn once again, and at last set out for the hunt.

The African twilight is sudden, and the sun drops in the west in an almost perfectly vertical line. Already there's no longer enough light to bother taking pictures. The lionesses move forward about ten yards, stop, and lower their heads to sniff the ground.

A male lion will often sniff a female's urine and make an expression that suggests a smile. Here the females smile faintly, too. Then they stretch out their forelegs, lower their hips and, though it's hard to see with certainty in the fading light, apparently make a soft stool. When a lion defecates in this way, it usually indicates not that she has diarrhea but that she has recently eaten fresh meat.

Perhaps this, too, is all part of their pre-hunt warm-up.

Early the next morning, we encounter the lionesses with their bellies bulging. Their faces seem content, almost lazy. Several spotted hyenas surround them at a distance. It could be that the lions stole the hyenas' catch last night. Spotted hyenas are excellent hunters, so this sort of thing happens often.

After returning home from Africa, the day at last arrives when I sit down with Shuji and designer Keisuke Konishi and begin to select pictures from an enormous pile to use in this book. The work continues for several days.

"Here's one."

"Nice color, isn't it?"

"The shape of this one is extraordinary, don't you think?"

"No, this one's much better."

It's a job that requires patience, but we enjoy ourselves; it's like searching for treasure.

After narrowing the choices down to 200 photographs, we decide to leave the final decisions to Keisuke. Keisuke manages to capture the instincts of these wild animals with a clever sense of rhythm, creating a refreshing composition. For the title of the book, we readily agree on the term that came up in our conversation in Frankfurt, "nature calls."

Nature Calls is a book concerning the "art" of the droppings and urine of wild animals. As you can see, each page portrays the gentle shapes and form of nature that I venture to call art. And all are created in the natural environment inhabited by wild animals.